THE FINAL GIRL: How Horror Movies made Me a Better Feminist
© Kris Rose, 2021, 2024
ISBN 9781648411106
This is Microcosm #691
This edition © Microcosm Publishing, 2021, 2024

For a catalog, write or visit:
Microcosm Publishing
2752 N Williams Ave.
Portland, OR 97227
www.Microcosm.Pub

To join the ranks of high-class stores that feature Microcosm titles, talk to your rep: In the U.S. **COMO** (Atlantic), **ABRAHAM** (Midwest), **BOB BARNETT** (Texas, Oklahoma, Arkansas, Louisiana), **IMPRINT** (Pacific), **TURNAROUND** (UK), **UTP/MANDA** (Canada), **NEWSOUTH** (Australia/New Zealand), **Observatoire** (Africa, Europe), **IPR** (Middle East), **Yvonne Chau** (Southeast Asia), **HarperCollins** (India), **Everest/B.K. Agency** (China), **Tim Burland** (Japan/Korea), and **FAIRE** and **EMERALD** in the gift trade.

Did you know that you can buy our books directly from us at sliding scale rates? Support a small, independent publisher and pay less than Amazon's price at www.Microcosm.Pub

Global labor conditions are bad, and our roots in industrial Cleveland in the 70s and 80s made us appreciate the need to treat workers right. Therefore, our books are MADE IN THE USA.

TABLE OF CONTENTS

INTRODUCTION

When I was thirteen, my mom began dating a man named John who had two kids. Richard was the oldest at nineteen, and John's daughter Carrie was just a few months younger than myself. John moved in after only a few months and brought both his kids with him. Since there were limited bedrooms in our house, it was decided that I would share my room with Carrie. I didn't mind, in fact it was fun having a "sister" my own age. Luckily, my new sister also enjoyed scaring the shit out of herself and we formed our own private movie club. Richard was allowed to join, but he had no say over what movies we picked, that was mostly my job. Being the boss over what movies people watched felt like a natural position, one I still aspire to today. My husband can tell you that I love nothing more than telling people what movies they should be watching or what books they should be reading. This eventually led to me opening my own bookstore with an ill-fated video rental section. I thought other geeks would jump at the chance to rent an obscure horror movie on VHS, but I was wrong. Apparently I was the only one left in Tulsa that felt nostalgia for the experience of browsing the covers at my local video store.

At thirteen, I was desperately searching out the few precious cultural markers that would lead me out of my small-minded and isolated hometown, and into the world of artists and weirdos where I felt I belonged. It was as if I was cramming for a test that I would be given someday in order to enter into the kingdom of cool. Every book, band, movie, or scrap of culture I could collect was a lifeline to keep me going long enough to escape my prison of childhood, trapped in a town I hated in a house that was not a home.

I loved all kinds of movies, and introduced my new sister to such dark classics as ***A Clockwork Orange*** (totally traumatized me), ***Heathers*** (which I bought on VHS and watched fifty times), and ***Cry-Baby*** (my first exposure to what would become a lifelong love of John Waters), but horror movies were the thing that my sister and I loved best. When we all lived together in Bixby, a small town thirty minutes south of Tulsa, we would get to rent movies and order pizza whenever our parents went out for date night. My own personal favorite video store of all time was in Bixby.

Showtime Video had a small room specifically dedicated to horror movies. This room seemed magical to me as a kid, separated from the rest of the store by the obligatory beaded curtain and decorated with large cut out displays of Freddy or Jason propped in the corners. The fake cobwebs semi-obscured the large, movie-theater-sized posters of classic 80s horror movies. Red light bulbs overhead made everything that much spookier and somehow enticing inside the room, but also made everything brighter and somewhat boring in the rest of the store, not to mention in the outside world in general. When I would finally exit that room twenty minutes later, I would do so in a daze, clutching my stack of choices like a life preserver in an ocean of shit.

While living with my dad I could walk there during the summer and rent anything I wanted to, since he was at work and the owners knew me well enough not to question my getting rated R movies at eleven years of age. One of the benefits of having a dad who paid zero attention to what was going on with me. When I was just about to enter the fifth grade, my friend Jennifer and I rented ***The Exorcist*** one summer afternoon and ruined ourselves for the next several years, but I have no regrets. Watching ***The Exorcist*** much too young and being totally fucked up by it forever was a right of passage for many kids of the 80s. On the bright side, it made every other horror movie seem less scary by comparison. After ***The Exorcist***, I became the baddest girl at the slumber party. Nothing scared me anymore. If it wasn't ***The Exorcist*****,** it wasn't shit to me.

In this time period of horror movie abundance, we discovered such masterpieces as ***The Evil Dead*** and ***Evil Dead 2*****,** and I became infatuated with Bruce Campbell. Carrie and I were at the first showing of ***Army of Darkness*** when it opened in Tulsa. I didn't care that he was old, or that I was thirteen, all I knew was that I loved him. When other teen girls were talking about New Kids on the Block, I was talking about Bruce Campbell. It did not endear me to other girls my age and probably made the adults in my life feel slightly uncomfortable as well.

Then came ***The Texas Chainsaw Massacre 2*****,** which almost took ***Evil Dead*****'S** place as our number one favorite movie to quote. Carrie and I began quoting Bill Moseley's character, Chop-Top, endlessly. Our parents were only mildly concerned to hear their thirteen-year-old daughters screaming "Lick my plate you dog dick!" across the house on any given evening.

My mom was happily distracted by John, who didn't work due to his pending workman's comp case, but who knew how to work the system. Thanks to John and

Catholic charities, we ate a lot of off-brand foods, cereal in pillowcase-sized bags, and in a good week, other people's messed up birthday cakes. It was a happier time for many reasons, mostly because I had step-siblings living with me who were near my own age. My blood siblings, as much as I loved them, were ten and twelve years older than myself and had long moved out by my thirteenth birthday. Because my mom was distracted, I was able to escape her micromanaging and constant focus on all the things I did wrong on a daily basis. That was John's cross to bear now. Plus, my mom hated all other women on some basic level, and my new step-sister was no exception. Carrie pulled some of the focus of my mother's anger, much to my relief. Since I had started to develop into a woman, my mother's resentment towards me was growing every day. Unlike my older sister, who was more reserved and avoided confrontation, I was a mouthy little shit. I refused to accept that my mother was smarter or knew what she was doing, because it was obvious to me that neither of those things were true. I know this is what all teenage girls think about their mothers at some point, but I happened to be right. I was only counting the days until I could escape my mother and Bixby, and horror movies were my salvation until then.

My love of horror only grew with time. I could relate to the main characters, almost always women, who had to survive a shitty situation using nothing but their wits and determination. They were often scared the majority of the movie, but they didn't let that fear stop them from doing what they had to do.

When Carrie and I were fifteen, her father moved into an apartment in Tulsa and I spent the majority of my time there also. My mom and John were still dating, but after a failed attempted move to Oregon together, she didn't invite him back into our home. When he crawled back to Tulsa only a few months after her own reluctant return, he moved into an apartment off of Cherry Street, right around the corner from Sound Warehouse, a record and video store that would become a fixture in my life. John and Carrie's reappearance into our lives was a relief. I was stuck alone in the house with my mother, but at least now I had an escape hatch to Tulsa whenever I wanted one.

Carrie and I began doing all the things rebellious fifteen year-olds do: sneaking cigarettes from her dad, stalking boys, and asking for spare change down at the local Texaco. We had a set amount of money we had to earn in order to buy our daily list of supplies: a large fountain Dr. Pepper, two bags of ranch flavored corn nuts, plus the rental fee for the "rent one, get one free" movies at Sound Warehouse. We only ever rented horror movies, and some pretty bad ones at that, but there was a comfort in the horrible things that happened on screen. It was a mirror of the horrible things that could happen in real life. For a girl whose life was not perfect, not even close to the artificial sweetness of 90s sitcoms, horror was a reassurance that darkness was a normal part of life. It was possible to survive the absolute worst, if you learned a few valuable lessons from one of the most well known archetypes of modern horror: The Final Girl.

THE FINAL GIRL (AND OTHER TROPES)

The Final Girl is a trope in horror films, particularly slasher films. It refers to the last girl or woman alive to confront the killer, ostensibly the one left to tell the story.

Slasher movies are where you usually find the most horror movie tropes that involve the "Final Girl."

Joss Whedon elaborated on these tropes in his screenplay for the 2012 film ***Cabin in the Woods,*** directed by Drew Goddard, which breaks down each teen protagonist into a category, or archetype. The types are: the Virgin, the Athlete, the Whore, the Fool, and the Scholar.

This follows what we all know to be true when we watch a ***Friday the 13th*** or Halloween-type slasher movie. We can spot each type and know from the first ten minutes or so that so-and-so will be dead before the halfway point. There are also very few minorities or gay characters in most slasher films, and fewer who survive 'til the end. The usual line up of young, white, healthy teens are as follows:

There's the "Slutty Girl," who is sexually aggressive, scantily clad, and usually dies in the throes of passion along with her boyfriend, usually the "dumb jock" of the group.

The Jock, or "Athlete," who can either be the final girl's love interest, or the boyfriend of the slutty girl, and can either be nice or a jerk, depending on how long we want him to survive. The jerk usually dies sooner than the nice guy, and sometimes the nice guy even manages to survive alongside the Final Girl, but not often.

There's the joker character, The Fool, usually an outsider, who either does drugs and/or subscribes to some sort of counterculture like punk, goth, or hippie.

There's the nerd, or The Scholar, who usually tries to warn his friends of impending doom. Sometimes this is substituted by a female character who simply functions as a Cassandra in the film. The Cassandra complex is a term for when people, usually women, predict disaster and are ignored or dismissed. The term originates with the French philosopher Gaston Bachelard in 1949, but the inspiration comes from Greek mythology. Cassandra was the daughter of Priam, king of Troy. She was so charming that Apollo bestowed upon her the gift of prophecy. However, when she refused his romantic advances, Apollo turned that gift into a curse by ensuring that nobody would ever believe her. She knew the terrible outcome of the Trojan War, but could do nothing to change future events.

Then, of course, you have your "Final Girl." She is the girl who survives it all and defeats the bad guy. Usually, the Final Girl is classified as a "Virgin," but hardly ever is that true in a literal sense. Movies such as ***Scream*** made much of the fact that their Final Girl, Sydney Prescott, lost her virginity during the course of the film and still managed to slay the murderers, but the mistake they made was to confuse "innocent" for "virginal." The Final Girl often has an air of innocence of spirit and heart about her, but that does not make her a virgin as such, simply naive about the darker side of life. It's her air of vulnerability and relatability that makes us root for her. Perhaps her life has been perfectly normal up until the events that shape her into a survivor, but more often, in the best horror movies, the relatable Final Girl already has troubles brewing at home, and the terrifying events are simply a catalyst to strengthen an already strong but struggling girl. When we want a Final Girl to survive, it ramps up the tension, and makes the entire movie better. That's why cheap imitators often make for entertaining one-time watches, but they never become the classics of the genre whose relevance endures over decades.

Some of the best Final Girls already have steady boyfriends when the film begins. Nancy Thompson in ***A Nightmare on Elm Street*** is already in a long term and loving relationship with Glenn, who also happens to live across the street from her. We see that he is easily able to climb the trellis outside her bedroom window, and we also know her mother drinks too much. No sane person would believe that, in those circumstances, these two attractive teenagers aren't already having sex.

It's true that Nancy rebuffs Glenn's advances while they're at Tina's house, but it's the circumstances that bother Nancy, not the fact of having sex itself. Nancy is very easily able to tell Glenn that "we're not here for that, we're here for Tina," and Glenn sleeps on the couch without argument. The fact that Nancy is able to confidently and unapologetically explain her boundaries without shame or remorse, and that Glenn accepts these boundaries without the whining or bargaining you sometimes see in teen movies of all genres, proves this film is above the tropes.

There is a similar scene in ***Night of the Demons*** where our Final Girl, Judy, is setting boundaries with her date Jay, who, it turns out, only asked her out because he thought she was easy. When she explains to him that not only did she not sleep with her last boyfriend but that she only went out with him once, he replies "Once is all it takes!" Judy reaffirms her position that she won't sleep with Jay under the current circumstances, but never explicitly says that she wouldn't sleep with him in the future after they had been dating longer, or that the reason she didn't sleep with her last date was because she was a virgin. Judy didn't sleep with her last boyfriend simply because he was never really her boyfriend. They only went out once, which was too soon for her in those circumstances. Jay storms off in a huff after Judy turns him down. She does try calling after him in a pleading tone, but he doesn't engage with her any further, as he's now done with her.

The character of Kirsty in the ***Hellraiser*** movies is most definitely not a virgin, and even has sex on the first date with a new boyfriend (Steve) that she meets at her dad's dinner party. This is not used against her in any way during the movie's plot. Her sexuality, such as it is, seems wholesome compared to the depravity of her Uncle Frank, whose need for kinkier sex has led him straight to Hell, literally.

Of course, Ripley of the ***Alien*** franchise is a grown ass woman. (And yes, she is also a Final Girl, and ***Alien*** and ***Aliens*** are horror movies. Ridley Scott himself has said that he was inspired by the first ***Texas Chainsaw Massacre*** movie and that, in fact, ***Alien*** is "***Texas Chainsaw Massacre*** in space"). Yes, she does own a cat, but that does not make her a spinster. She has crazy sexual chemistry with Hicks, for one, and two, in the beginning of ***Aliens,*** the sequel to ***Alien***, Ripley finds out that her daughter Amanda has died while Ripley was in stasis for fifty-seven years. This definitely makes her not a virgin. It's interesting to note as well that in ***Aliens*** she loses her space flight license due to her superiors' disbelief of her horrifying story of survival. In ***Aliens,*** Ripley acts as her own Cassandra. Her warnings about the aliens go unheeded, and predictably disaster ensues, but she is unable to prevent it.

The only certified virgin of our group is ***Halloween*'s** Laurie Strode. She's a straight-A student, acting as her own "Scholar" archetype. Laurie Strode is probably the most famous Final Girl because she is considered by many to be the first. Many people see ***Halloween*** as the first slasher movie. While I concede that it is definitely the "Cadillac of slasher films," as Bruce Campbell put it, there's an argument to be made that ***Texas Chainsaw Massacre*** would be the first official slasher that followed the tropes.

THE MOVIES THAT SCARRED/ SCARED ME AND BECAME SACRED TO ME

Texas Chainsaw Massacre

1974

Directed by Tobe Hooper

Starring Marilyn Burns, Gunnar Hansen, Teri McMinn, Paul A. Partain, Edwin Neal, and Jim Siedow

If Rob Zombie is correct in his assertion that "slasher movies were when the killer became the star," Leatherface definitely meets that criterion. There are only a handful of bad guys as recognizable as Leatherface. Sally Hardesty is our first Final Girl by definition, but she's a far cry from the serious and determined Laurie. Sally definitely falls in the woods while trying to run from Leatherface, but to be fair, she is running through thick underbrush in total darkness while being chased by a giant man with a chainsaw.

Sally is barely there personality-wise, but we still root for her to get into the truck bed and get away from Leatherface by the end of the film. What we do know about her is that she's willing to jump out of a window twice in order to survive, which shows determination. Many people would simply give up and let the worst happen to them rather than take a risk like jumping through glass—*twice*! When Tobe Hooper was asked about this directorial choice, he said that most movies would have a character jump through a window once, but never twice in the same film, so he was gonna do it because no audience would expect it. To his credit, I have to say that it definitely makes an impact in the way it telegraphs to viewers how determined Sally is to survive this horrific experience at all costs.

As much as ***Texas Chainsaw Massacre*** was one of the first of its kind, and an innovative horror film, director Tobe Hooper had two major inspirations for the film. One being the famous Wisconsin Ghoul Ed Gein, who dug up the bodies of dead women and made objects from the body parts, and two, the 1960 film ***Psycho***, directed by Alfred Hitchcock.

Psycho

1960

Directed by Alfred Hitchcock

Starring Anthony Perkins, Janet Leigh, Vera Miles, John Gavin, and Pat Hitchcock

In ***Psycho***, Norman Bates, played to perfection by Anthony Perkins, steals the body of his dead mother before it can be buried, and preserves it in his home using taxidermy chemicals. He also occasionally dresses up like his mother, wearing her old dresses and a wig, and acts out violently whenever he's sexually aroused. This violent acting out happens when Norman is sexually aroused by our heroine, Marion Crane (played by Janet Leigh, who's the mother of actress Jamie Leigh Curtis, who stars in ***Halloween*** as Laurie Strode). When Marion dies forty minutes into the film, we are then introduced to her sister, and, if ***Psycho*** were to have one, our true Final Girl, Lila Crane.

The original ***Psycho*** was controversial for many reasons. In 1960, the Hays Code (adopted in 1930 but not taken seriously until 1934) was beginning to lose its thirty-year-long hold on the movie industry. This code was a set of guidelines that decided what could or could not be seen on screen. It was finally done away with entirely in favor of the ratings system in 1968, which is why the 1970s was such an amazing decade for cinema.

Hitchcock had to fight for the inclusion of many scenes that wouldn't even raise an eyebrow these days. The opening shot showing Marion in a bra and slip, lying in the same bed as her boyfriend, was quite controversial. Showing unmarried couples in the same bed was a big taboo, in fact many TV shows had married couples sleeping in twin beds several feet apart from each other until ***The Flintstones*** showed Fred and Wilma in the same bed in 1960.

One scene that was particularly troubling to the censors was one of Marion throwing torn up pieces of paper down the toilet and the pieces being flushed. No flushing toilet had ever been seen on film before and it scandalized the censors. As tough as American censors were, the British censors were tougher, and many cuts (pun intended) had to be made to the shower scene before the film could be shown in Great Britain.

As much as ***Psycho*** has influenced every slasher film that's come after it, there is one other film that was released a few months earlier that stands as a real contender for the title of first-ever slasher. It's a movie called ***Peeping Tom***, directed by Michael Powell and written by Leo Marks. I won't get into the plot here, but it's definitely worth checking out.

Texas Chainsaw Massacre 2

1986

Directed by Tobe Hooper

Starring Dennis Hopper, Bill Mosely, Caroline Williams, Jim Siedow, and Lou Perryman

Comparing Sally in the first ***Texas Chainsaw Massacre*** to Vanita "Stretch" Brock in ***Texas Chainsaw Massacre 2***, is like comparing apples to oranges. The years in between the two films gave writer and director Tobe Hooper enough time to develop a stronger Final Girl. We don't get tons of teenagers dying on screen, but I think in their own ways, the deaths in TCM2 are just as powerful, if not more so. The deaths in the sequel are either ones we're rooting for (rich dicks at the beginning of the film, Chop-Top at the end of the film) or are truly sad ones, (L.G., Franklin's skeleton still in his wheelchair, Lefty going down with the ship, so to speak.) and hold more emotional weight than the ones in the first film.

The character of Vanita "Stretch" Brock is one of my very favorite Final Girls. During the course of the opening scene she goes from being annoyed by some preppie assholes who call into her radio show to being horrified by what she hears, as they meet their demise at the hands of maniacs with a chainsaw.

She then actively tracks down Dennis Hopper's character "Lefty," in order to help him catch his niece and nephew's legendary tormentors (his niece and nephew being Sally and Franklin from the first film), who she suspects may be the same people she heard murdering her callers over the phone.

When Leatherface and his brother Chop-Top do show up at the radio station in order to quiet her after she replays the recorded murder of the obnoxious football preps, she is shaken to her core and nearly murdered herself. Leatherface has her cornered and she should end up dead, except for the fact that she realizes the maniac wielding the chainsaw is just as dumb and horny as any other Texas man. She then manages to flirt with Leatherface despite her own fear and her quick thinking saves her life. Even when she's safe from her near-death encounter, the thought of the murderers getting away prompts her to follow them to their hideout, and by not showing up on time, Lefty leaves her to follow them all alone.

Once she enters the hideout, she discovers that there's an entire family behind the murders. The local chili champion Drayton Sawyer (the amazing John Seidow reprising his role from the first film) is the ringleader and public face of the family BBQ business. This award winning BBQ champion happens to be using human flesh brought to him by Leatherface and Chop-Top, to be sold for consumption by unsuspecting customers.

Lefty, brilliantly played by Dennis Hopper (even though subsequently he said it was one of the worst movies he'd ever been in), finally shows up just in time to scare the shit out of Stretch, which causes her to fall into the heart of the macabre underground bunker the family has fashioned inside of a deserted, Texas-themed family attraction. While there, she has to endure the discovery that her sweet and loyal sidekick, L.G., has fallen victim to Leatherface and has had his own face removed and made into a mask, which she then has to wear in order to keep Leatherface from killing her too. The scene where L.G. uses the last bit of his strength to free Stretch before succumbing to his wounds is strangely touching. Stretch takes a moment amongst all the horror to mourn his death, and you actually feel for her. This is probably because Lou Perryman made L.G. such a loveable character, and Caroline Williams really sells every bit of her performance. The realistic way in which she portrays Stretch as constantly screaming and terrified makes her an even better heroine. It's not that Stretch isn't scared shitless by these monsters, she's clearly freaking out the entire movie, but she does the brave thing despite being so terrified. In the end, she fights for her life and wins, bringing down the entire twisted clan by wielding the chainsaw as adeptly as Leatherface himself. Her victory swings with the chainsaw echo the ending of the original ***Chainsaw Massacre***, and we are left wondering if she has been driven past the point of sanity by it all, but we're also kind of psyched to see her go ape shit with a chainsaw.

Why Stretch Is a True Heroine

1. She cares about what's right, not what's easy

Even though the football-loving rich dicks who try and fuck with her on her own radio show are probably the last people on Earth most people would want to defend, Stretch goes out of her way to find their murderers. She tracks down Lefty after reading an unflattering newspaper article about his plight, an article that basically makes fun of him and tries to make the possibility of a chainsaw-wielding mass murderer into a joke. She thinks her phone experience with the jocks could be connected somehow. The cops don't want to mess with it, and even Lefty is reluctant to try again after so many disappointments, but Stretch persists, because in her mind these killers need to be brought to justice.

2. "Don't call me darlin'!"

Even though she loves and adores L.G., she still corrects him whenever he tries to act paternal towards her by calling her "darlin'" Stretch realizes that a seemingly harmless term of affection also carries with it the attitude that they aren't equals. L.G. can't think of her as a business partner and respected co-worker if he's acting paternally towards her in the workplace by thinking of her as a "little woman who needs to be protected." She proves quite the opposite over and over again in the movie, as each of the "aw shucks ma'am" male characters not only end up failing to protect her, but even end up putting her in harm's way.

3. She is selfless

Stretch follows the killers even after she escapes being murdered by Leatherface because she can't stand the thought of them getting away with murder. When Lefty and L.G. leave her alone to face the killers, she uses her smarts to con Leatherface into letting her go. After almost getting cut up with a chainsaw, most people would promptly pack everything they own and leave town forever, but not Stretch. She knows that if she lets them get away, many more people will die, and that's something she can't live with. She sees it as her duty to follow them and make sure that they're somehow stopped from hurting anyone else. Could she have planned a little better? Probably, but we can give her a little slack—she *is* in the middle of being traumatized for life, after all.

Lines from TCM2 that my 13-year-old step sister and I used way too often

1. Chop-top: "Lick my plate you dog dick!"
2. Chop-Top: "Dog will hunt, get that bitch!"
3. L.G.: "Looky, made you lil fry house!" (and can I just add that if some man made me a "lil' house" out of french fries, I would marry him on the spot?)
4. Chop-top: "Did you see the size of that booger?" Drayton: "What booger?" Chop-top: "Big craaaazy booger!"

Lessons learned from Vanita "Stretch" Brock

1. Listen to good music like the Cramps and The Ramones
2. Sometimes you can charm dangerous men into leaving you alone
3. Doing the brave thing doesn't mean you're not also scared
4. What's good for the chainsaw-wielding goose is also good for the gander
5. Never rely on anyone named "Lefty."

Waxwork

1988

Written and directed by Anthony Hickox

Starring Zach Galligan, Deborah Foreman, Michelle Johnson, and Dana Ashbrook

A group of high school friends get invited to a midnight showing at a waxworks museum that mysteriously appears in a neighborhood overnight.

First Scene that got my attention:Mark, (played by Zach Galligan) plays a rich boy who's just been rejected by the hot girl, China (played by Michelle Johnson.) While at a party with friends, he confronts her about ditching him the night before to go hang out with a hunky jock. To this China responds, "I do what I want, when I want. Dig it or fuck off!"

I have to say that watching her assert her independence was inspiring to me at the tender age of eleven. She was cool, mouthy, sophisticated, beautiful, and more than a little pretentious with her black turtlenecks and use of the term "je ne sais quoi," when referring to what exactly it was she was looking for in a man. As much as I wanted her to be the heroine of the movie, I knew she was doomed. Not because she was open about her sexuality, but because she was reckless and arrogant, two things you couldn't be if you wanted to survive a horror movie.

This brings us to our actual heroine and Final Girl, Sarah (played by the amazing Deborah Foreman, who also famously starred in ***Valley Girl*** and ***April Fool's Day***). She is obviously set up to be our Final Girl, because she's more conservatively dressed than China, shows some amount of hesitation when invited into a museum at midnight by a strange man dressed in Willy Wonka drag, and has a reserved but unspoken crush on our main guy, Mark. Add to the mix the dumb hot guy, Tony (played by professional dumb hot guy of ***Twin Peaks*** fame, Dana Ashbrook), and another couple, Gemma and James, who are really only there to fill out the numbers needed for the master plan of our villian.

Even though this film follows some of the rules of 80s horror, it also breaks them in some very surprising ways. For instance, China doesn't meet her demise because of her love of sex, but because she's mistaking dangerous for interesting when it comes to life. She's bored by the banality of her everyday existence, so she dabbles with the angry jock and jumps at the invitation of an obviously suspicious man in the hopes of making her life more interesting. When she is finally confronted with having to fight for her life, she does an admirable job up until the final moment, when she is confronted by the seductive head vampire himself. All the fight goes out of her as she immediately surrenders to his killing bite, a disappointing end to a fun character, but pretty standard for this type of female character in most horror movies.

Just look at Trash in ***Return of the Living Dead***; she drunkenly exclaims her fantasy of being devoured by a group of strange old men, and mere moments later she's literally being devoured by a gang of rotting male zombies. Expressing sexual desires in horror movies for women can be fatal. We believe ourselves to be watching just another sexually aggressive woman getting her monkey's paw version of her sexual fantasies fulfilled, par for the course, but then we get to Sarah in ***Waxwork.*** It's she who subverts the normal storyline in two ways. Number one, she is finally seen to be the girl worthy of our main guy's affections after he gives up on trying to get back with the ever-elusive China. In this scene, it's expected that Sarah will be grateful that Mark has finally noticed her, but instead we get a very sweet exchange between the two characters even though Sarah basically rejects Mark, our "hero." She tells him that, while she finds him very attractive, she's looking for something else. When she begins to feel bad about rejecting Mark, he reassures her that she shouldn't worry about it, and that he still thinks she's great. From then on, the two leads are friends who help and support each other and do so without judgement. Later on in the movie we see that Sarah has a thing for the Marquis De Sade, and when she enters into the wax display and is willingly whipped almost to death by him, Mark helps her come to her senses, but does so without making her feel bad or guilty for being into some heavy S&M. This was a pretty sweet curveball the movie threw into the mix. Having the "good girl" be way into some kinky bondage shit was pretty mind blowing. In fact, she makes our previous "bad girl" China look pretty vanilla by comparison. So Mark does save the day, or at least lends a hand in helping Sarah to save herself. Cliche right on track, or so we think. Later on in the movie we see that Sarah ends up saving Mark by slaying the very object of her desire, the Marquis De Sade, so she effectively has the last word, the last heroic act, the part that usually goes to the man in a "couple who survives till the end" finale. It's worth noting that the director, Anthony Hickox, was dating actress Deborah Foreman when he wrote the script, specifically with her in mind for the role of Sarah. Perhaps he gave her such a complex character as a sort of love letter.

Lessons learned

1. Saying "dig it or fuck off!" sounds cool when China says it, weirdly innapropriate when your eleven-year-old self says it.
2. The "good girl" can also have really kinky sexual fetishes and still be the good girl.
3. Sometimes you end up friends with a guy you used to crush on because even though you're attracted to them, there's not enough there for a relationship.
4. Real classy dudes will accept your rejection with grace and be your ride-or-die, even when they catch you trying to off yourself in a weird sex dungeon with a long since deceased historical figure.
5. A good girl with kinks can save the day, and her bro, and be the heroine of the story.

Hellraiser and Hellraiser 2

1987 and 1988

Directed by Tony Randel

Starring Andrew Robinson, Clare Higgins, Ashley Laurence, Doug Bradly Kenn, and Imogen Boorman

Hellraiser and its sequel don't follow the tropes of your average teenage slasher or "group of teens meet disaster" formula, but Kirsty and Tiffany were two of my favorite Final Girls growing up, which qualifies them for inclusion in this section.

Kirsty is one Final Girl that really goes through a true character arc throughout the first two ***Hellraiser*** movies. In the first one she's clever, but mostly terrified and confused. When her father and unlikeable step-mother Julia move back into the family home, they discover that the father's younger and much better looking brother, Frank, has been squatting there, apparently jerking off all over the place amongst a collection of ancient erotic artifacts and religious statues.

It is then revealed that Julia, the wicked step-mother, cheated on her husband Larry (Kirsty's father) on their wedding day with Frank years ago and has been lusting for him ever since. It turns out that Frank opened a box which unleashed S&M demons/angels to take him to another dimension, one he escapes from with the help of some dripping blood on the floorboards where he perished. This blood allows Frank to come back in partial form, mostly sinew and ooze. Still, he's able to convince a horrified, but still horny for him, Julia to bring strange men back to the attic so Frank can drain their life force and become whole once again.

The first man Julia brings home seems sort of sweet, right up until she starts to have some misgivings about what she's doing. He interprets her reluctance to murder him as her backing out of sex, which sends him into a rage and reveals him to be a total asshole. After a few more men, Julia begins to get a taste for murder, however she's still reluctant to let Frank murder her husband Larry.

Kirsty goes to check on Julia, at her father's behest, only to discover her bringing a man home. She enters the house thinking she's busting Julia for having an affair, but it's then revealed that her Uncle Frank is a monster hiding in her dad's attic, feeding off men lured in by Julia. She escapes Frank's sexual advances with the puzzle box in hand, and later opens it by accident in a hospital. It's there that she makes a deal with the demons/angels (otherwise known as cenobites) to serve them up Frank in exchange for her own freedom.

There's a final showdown at the house where Frank is recaptured after accidentally, but not too regretfully, killing Julia. Kirsty and her new boyfriend have one amazing moment where she's trying to solve the puzzle and send the cenobites back to Hell when Steve, the boyfriend, tries to "mansplain" to her how to move the puzzle. Kirsty yells "NO!" and pulls it out of his reach and does the job herself. It's a moment I never noticed until recently, and it's such a great moment. Here is this guy who is witnessing demons and death and magic all at once, but he's still trying to take over and be the boss of things even though he has no clue what's actually going on. Perhaps for this reason we don't see Steve again in the sequel.

Steve served the function of the "girlfriend" character, a character that's one dimensional and entirely disposable. We get his replacement, Kyle, in the sequel. He's blandly attractive and nice enough, but ultimately doomed. After the events of the first movie, we see that Kirsty has ended up in a psychiatric hospital run by a Dr. Channard, who (unbeknownst to his protegee Kyle, who is also a doctor) has an obsession with the occult. When Dr. Channard hears Kirsty's story about the box and the cenobites, he gets the police to deliver to his home the bloody mattress where Julia died. Kirsty claims that Julia can be brought back by using the mattress, so the doctor brings home a patient who believes he's covered in bugs and gives him a straight razor. The patient begins to cut himself while sitting on the mattress, and the blood brings a now skinless Julia back to life. All of this is witnessed by Kyle, who was hiding in the room the entire time. He then sneaks out to go warn Kirsty and help her escape the hospital. However, while there, she's visited by the bloody corpse of what she believes to be her father, causing her to go directly to Dr. Channard's home in the hopes she can somehow rescue her father from Hell. Kyle agrees to go with her, because he's blandly "nice," but don't get too attached, the men in ***Hellraiser*** aren't the main characters. In the meantime, Dr. Channard has sacrificed many of his patients to feed Julia and bring her back to her former skin-having glory. He also brings home a special mute patient named Tiffany, who has a particular fascination with solving puzzles. The doctor has quite the collection of occult items, including three different puzzle boxes of the same type used in the first film. He sets Tiffany down with one and lets her try to solve it while he and Julia hide behind a two-way mirror and watch. Predictably, Tiffany solves the puzzle box, opening the doorways to Hell, but is spared by the cenobites because they can sense it was the

Doctor who brought them there with his desire to know the reality of Hell. Kyle ends up being fed on by Julia, sorry Kyle. This leaves Dr. Channard, Julia, Tiffany, and Kirsty to walk into a Hell-type dimension, which looks like a vast labyrinth with a floating geometric shape known as Leviathan, Lord of the Labyrinth, God of chaos and desire, ruler and creator of the cenobites.

In "Hell," Kirsty confronts her creepy Uncle Frank, who tricked her into thinking he was her father who needed help. She pretends to go along with his wishes, which seems to be to have an incestuous relationship with his niece, but instead sets his chamber of Hell on fire, burning his skin away, leaving him a disgusting skinless monster once more. Enter Julia, with Tiffany. Frank attempts to boss Julia around like he did on Earth, but she's over it. She promptly rips his heart out, literally, and snipes back the same phrase he used when he killed her in the first movie, "Nothing personal, babe."

Even though Julia is supposed to be evil, you can't help but like her. In fact, both she and Kirsty are the only people worth rooting for in the entire series.

Although the second film relies on some pretty cheesy claymation effects and trite one-liners, it still has some undeniable appeal and charm. Some of the visual effects are laughable while others are breathtakingly gross. It's an odd mix. Kirsty becomes stronger throughout the movie, especially when she is protecting Tiffany. Where Julia was a wicked step-mother in life and an Evil Queen in Hell to Kirsty, Kirsty herself becomes a protective and loving mother figure to Tiffany, who we are to assume is now motherless thanks to some brief and confusing flashbacks. It is when the two girls join forces, with Tiffany's puzzle solving skills and Kirsty's quick thinking, that the girls are able to escape Julia, Dr. Channard, and the cenobites. The ending of the film is something of a mess. I won't get into the details, but I will outline my main takeaways from the film.

Lessons learned

1. Blandly attractive and helpful guys are fine, but nothing to get worked up about.
2. Helping others who are in your same terrible situation can often be a way to heal yourself and can often make you stronger.
3. Darkness can shrivel you up and make you cold, or it can make you empathize with others who have also been through something terrible.

Reasons Kirsty is a Bad-Ass

1. She never relies on any of her nice but blandly attractive boyfriends to help her out of her situation.
2. Even after everything she's been through, when her father asks for her help, her automatic response is, I need to get to Hell ASAP and save my dad. I have two fathers, a biological one and a step-father, and I don't like either of them enough to go to Quick Trip for them, let alone Hell.
3. She barely knows Tiffany, but she tries to protect her even when it puts her own life in danger.
4. She negotiates her way out of torture with sex demons and wins.
5. NO -- *STEVE!* For the last time! She doesn't need help figuring out the puzzle box

*Friday the 13th*_

1980

Directed by Sean S. Cunningham

Starring Betsy Palmer, Adrienne King, Harry Crosby, Laurie Bartram, Mark Nelson, Jeannine Taylor, Robbi Morgan, and Kevin Bacon

This is known for its more-than-human slasher Jason Voorhees. However, in the first ***Friday the 13th*** film, the killer is revealed to be the mother of Jason, who drowned as a boy in Crystal Lake because the camp counselors were off having sex instead of watching him. So technically, one of the first and most famous slashers ended up being a middle aged woman who killed teens in order to avenge the death of her son. And honestly, what middle-aged woman hasn't wanted to murder a bunch of obnoxious teenagers? I know the closer I get to 50, the more I want to.

I didn't watch ***Friday the 13th*** movies very much as a kid, it didn't grab me the same way the ***Nightmare on Elm Street*** or ***Halloween*** movies did. I think that has to do with the strong Final Girls in those other franchises. However, after seeing some clips from ***Friday the 13th, Part 4*** of Crispin Glover dancing, I might give at least this one movie in the franchise a second look.

A Nightmare on Elm Street 1

1984

Directed and Written by Wes Craven

Starring Robert Englund, Heather Langenkamp, Johnny Depp, John Saxon, Amanda Wyss, and Ronee Blakely

Wes Craven's daughter observed, when watching his movie ***Swamp Thing***, that she hated how women always tripped and fell while running away from their attackers in horror movies. He made a mental note of this and decided to make his female characters stronger in the future. This manifested in 1984's ***A Nightmare on Elm Street*** in the character of Nancy Thompson.

The unusual thing about the character of Nancy is that she never seems to suffer from self-doubt. Nancy is very strong willed and confident in the things that she knows and the choices she makes. Getting to the truth of the matter is the most important thing to her, because she senses that there's more to the truth than people are telling her, especially her parents. Nancy sees in her parents the hypocrisy of keeping up appearances. Her parents are divorced and clearly very troubled, but they choose to present themselves as normal, upstanding citizens. Nancy needs to get to the bottom of things. Nancy's mom even tells her point blank "You face things. That's your nature; that's your gift. Sometimes you have to turn away too."

Most people would be happy to brush the ugly truth under the rug and pretend it wasn't happening. As the movie progresses, everyone in Nancy's life, including and especially her boyfriend Glenn's parents, think that she is going crazy. Glenn's dad specifically says that he "doesn't want that lunatic hanging out with our kid anymore." Nancy starts out as an everyday American girl, but turns into an outcast. Glenn's dad even prevents Nancy from waking Glenn up in time to save his life. Glenn's dad fears Nancy's otherness and her possible contamination of his son more than the actual threat, which is Freddy. The fact that Freddy is only targeting these children because of the sins of their parents translates nicely to real life parental denial. Parents almost never think the danger to their kids comes from sources close to home, instead they blame "other" causes from outside. Glenn's dad causes his own son's death at the hands of Freddy Krueger multiple times, first with his vigilantism, and secondly by isolating him from the one person who can truly understand what he's going through and actually save him from the source of real danger. Often teens are separated from each other because the parents blame their group of friends for their bad behavior, when in reality having companionship with peers to whom they can relate is often a life saver. When teens fail to meet the expectations of their parents, the blame is often shifted to the culture that teens are consuming at the time (think of Ozzy Osborne, Twisted Sister, and the Satanic Panic of the 80s), especially when the real problems are caused by the parents themselves.

*A Nightmare on Elm Street 3: Dream Warriors*_

1987

Directed by Chuck Russell

Written by: Wes Craven, Bruce Wagner and Frank Darabont

Starring: Robert Englund, Heather Langenkamp, Patricia Arquette, Jennifer Rubin, Craig Wasson, Laurence Fishburne and Priscilla Pointer

Dream Warriors continues the theme of the Elm Street movies, which in essence are about the powerlessness of being a teenager: to go through a trauma and not be believed by your parents, authority figures, doctors, or the police. Growing up in an abusive household when there wasn't really a term for emotional abuse, I knew exactly what it was like to not be believed. Every time the cops came to my house, I tried to tell them that my mom was abusive, but instead of validation, they'd always ask to see proof of the abuse. I often couldn't show them any bruises because the thing had just happened or physical violence hadn't occurred. They would tell me in no uncertain terms that they could take me out of my house, but that I would only end up in foster care. They made sure I knew that foster care could be so much worse than where I was currently. The term "the devil you know" wasn't one I was familiar with until years later, but I knew the concept by heart from a very young age.

Watching the teens in the hospital setting of ***Dream Warriors*** struggle with real life problems, on top of the supernatural ones, helped me with my own struggles. I identified with the characters so much, that around the age of nine or ten, I convinced my dad to buy me a book all about the first three ***Nightmare on Elm Street*** movies while at the mall. The book detailed the plots of the movies, but also went into behind the scenes details about how they did certain special effects. I was fascinated. Knowing how things were done made them less frightening to me. However, when I brought the book with me to my mother's house, she immediately took it away from me and hid it in some unknown location. She claimed that it would "warp" me, her favorite term. She refused to listen to me or understand why the book was important to me. I have never to this day been able to find where she hid that book! It's worth something like fifty dollars now, so buying it again is not happening. I'm sure I'll find it someday when I'm clearing out her house.

Rewatching some of the special effects in this movie as an adult is sometimes sort of cringy, unlike rewatching the first *Nightmare on Elm Street*, which holds up surprisingly well for its age. Those special effects are solid and the character of Freddy seems much scarier. There are plenty of cheesy moments in ***Dream Warriors***, plenty of moments where you wonder who this movie is actually *for* because it almost seems to be aimed at kids. Though I must admit, I love a TV mohawk, and the character of Taryn sports one of the best in the business.

The character of Nancy becomes sort of a protector of these new kids, the last generation of Elm Street children. She especially forms a bond with the new Final Girl, Kristen. That relationship almost mirrors perfectly that of Kirsty and Tiffany in *Hellraiser*. Although, I think Wes Craven made a mistake when deciding to kill Nancy off at the end of ***Dream Warriors***. Kristen isn't nearly a strong enough character on her own, and Patricia Arquette, while charming in later movies, as much as I hate to say it, has a sort of whiny quality to her voice that makes her a little bit unlikeable. Nancy in this film isn't nearly as fearless, maybe due to the direction of Chuck Russell. She's still pretty ballsy and just as strong willed as before, however. There's a scene in which she's trying to rescue Joey from falling into a flaming pit and she hangs onto him for so long that she herself begins to go over the edge. Instead of letting him go, as most people would, she starts to fall into the pit as well. At the last second, she and Joey are pulled up to safety by Kincaid, but you get the feeling Nancy would have fallen to her death rather than give up her grip on Joey. That's first NOES Nancy in a nutshell.

I watched a short documentary called *I Am Nancy*, made by Heather Langenkamp, where she tries to talk to horror convention goons about what the character of Nancy means to them. Of course, the majority of men have Freddy tattoos and Freddy dolls and tons of merchandise geared towards celebrating a child molester who murdered children. I get it, Robert Englund is a charming and charismatic motherfucker. At every convention he attends he has a line going out the door and it's hours of waiting just to get a photo or an autograph, while Heather and the girl who played Alice in ***A Nightmare on Elm Street 4: The Dream Master*** have almost nobody in their lines. I think that's total bullshit. I think we need an all female horror convention where the Final Girls and the scream queens get all the attention, no Freddies allowed. A good thing that has happened because of Nancy is that Heather Langenkamp has said that her first real fans were young gay men who used Nancy as the inspiration for coming out of the closet to their families.

That, however, is not the only connection ***A Nightmare on Elm Street*** has to the gay community; there's also the homoerotic ***A Nightmare on Elm Street Two: Freddy's Revenge***, but that's a whole other chapter. In fact, I encourage you all to go find and watch the documentary called ***Scream Queen!: My Nightmare on Elm Street*** about the making of ***Freddy's Revenge***, made by the star of that movie, Mark Patton. If you haven't seen ***Freddy's Revenge***, I highly recommend you check it out, especially for the appearance of Tulsa's own Clu Gulager, a personal horror hero of mine. His son made a few amazing horror movies in the early 2000s; ***Feast*, *Feast 2*, and *Feast 3***, and all of them starred his amazing wife Diane Goldner. There's a scene in ***Feast 2*** that is probably one of the best/worst/funniest scenes that I've ever seen in any horror movie. I cannot ruin it for you by telling you what it is, but trust me that it is sick. And hilarious, and it breaks every rule of cinema morality. Or just human morality, but it's also so fucking real. You can tell he's from Tulsa by his sense of dark humor. Tulsans are the darkest motherfuckers when it comes to humor that I have ever met. I have a whole collection of stories that are just about hilarious things that have happened while at funerals. There's just a dark vein of humor that runs through this town. Either you get it or you don't, but my guess is that since you're reading this, you might be prone to dark humor.

Best Quotes

1. Nancy to Freddy: "I take back every bit of energy I ever gave you. You're nothing. You're s***!"
2. Nancy to mom: "MOTHER! What's with the bars?"
3. Nancy to mom: "Screw sleep!"
4. Glenn (who has to listen to Tina and Rod have sex after being rejected by Nancy): "Morality Sucks!"

Why Nancy is a Great Final Girl

1. She's the most ride-or-die of the bunch. If Nancy is your friend, or even just on your team, she would literally search the depths of Hell to rescue you.
2. She taught herself a bunch of *Rambo: First Blood* stuff in a day, while sleep deprived for a week. I can barely put my shoes on after losing a few hours of sleep.
3. After the death of her friends and mother, and being hounded by Freddy, she still manages to graduate from college and become a successful grad student who then trashes her entire promising career in order to save complete strangers.
4. She's an "average American girl" in most ways, but she has ugly and embarrassing real life problems, such as her mom's alcoholism. The roles of parent and child are almost reversed in a scene where Nancy puts her drunk and remorseful mother to bed, tucks her in and takes care of her at the time when Nancy herself needs the most help. In ***Dream Warriors*** she also plays a maternal role in Kristen's life. Kristen's actual mother is too busy trying to please the men in her life, and worries about appearances more than substance. The fact that Kristen comes from wealth was not something I immediately picked up on as a kid. All the homes in movies seemed nicer than mine, although I suspect that if we were to see Taryn's home, it would look a lot more familiar.

Night of the Demons

1988

Directed by Kevin S. Tenney

Starring Linnea Quigley, Amelia Kincaid, Cathy Podewell, Alvin Alexis, and Billy Gallo

One thing my husband noted right off the bat while watching this movie was that there's a diverse cast in this film compared to others of its era and type. Jill Terashita as Frannie, who plays a sort of valley girl, Billy Gallo as Sal, who plays more of a stereotypical New York Italian tough guy, and finally Alvin Alexis as Roger, who ends up being our final boy alongside our Final Girl, Cathy Podewell (who plays Judy). Roger does play into some well worn stereotypes: his daddy was a preacher, and he knows how to pray "real good," but unlike most Black characters in other horror movies who often end up being killed early on, Roger runs away at the first sign of danger while the dumb white people just stand there. Roger also gets to play the hero a few times to our Final Girl Judy, which is very unusual for a character of color in a horror film.

The list of things I love about this movie are endless, but we have limited time and I've used up most of it talking about the strongest Final Girls of my childhood. Judy is okay, but the girls I love in this film are B-A-D, namely scream queen Linnea Quigley as Suzanne and newcomer Amelia Kincaid as Angela, who does maybe the best thing in the whole movie—scaring the shit out of Sal with her newfound demon sexuality.

Female sexuality is used as a weapon more in this movie than any other of my childhood. The asshole Jay (the Jock who's a jerk) has just ditched Judy because she refused to have sex with him on the first date. He stumbles upon Suzanne, who is obviously not in a good way, but he's so blinded by his own need to get laid and Suzanne's boobs that he ignores every red flag being thrown at him. She has lipstick all over her face! They start to fool around and that's when the "fun" stuff happens.

Even though they're "demons," I still liked them better than the main characters who were trying to escape. I mean, for all the times Roger came through and saved Judy, there were more times when he screamed and ran away and generally acted like a little bitch. Don't get me wrong, I love a male Final Girl who screams and runs away and acts like a little bitch, that's almost entirely what Ash does throughout the ***Evil Dead*** movies, and we all know how I feel about Bruce Campbell. Linnea Quigley is well known in the horror world, she even came out with a horror themed work out video, which might be the only work out video in the world that I would ever do on a regular basis. I'm still waiting for a horror movie themed yoga video, but the closest I could find was a lady doing yoga in a brightly lit nightclub to Korn. Fucking NO! So I related to Angela more than Judy, but I still think NOTD gets credit for letting a person of color be the hero in a time when it was already a cliche that the person of color died first, or at least died, period.

THE RELATABILITY OF FINAL GIRLS

Relating to Carrie White

Speaking of movies in which I related to the bad girl, watching the movie ***Carrie*** as a young girl was also, no surprise, a big deal for me. I have to admit that I more than identify with the character of Carrie White, the victim as well as monster of Stephen King's *Carrie*. Living with a mother who is uncontrollably insane is no picnic. That's a fucking understatement. I was the girl at school whose weird mom would show up wearing strange or outdated clothing and scarves on her head like she was some sort of Eastern European refugee. I would have kids saying "Who's that lady? She looks weird! Why is she wearing a scarf?" and I would have to answer, "I don't know! I don't know why she does anything." That is when I wasn't running away, denying evnr knowing her or suggesting that she might be somebody else's mom, but definitely not mine.

Being torn about whether or not to stand up for your own mom because your mom is so shitty that she doesn't stand up for you is a bad feeling to have. One way to exorcise bad feelings is through catharsis, and for me that catharsis was horror movies. I loved horror movies from a *very* young age. They scared me, they traumatized me, but I always, always went back for more. I remember watching ***Gremlins*** alone in my trailer, (surprise—guess who grew up in a trailer park) knowing that I was going to get too scared, but doing it anyway. I would have my legs up on the cushion of the sofa (they couldn't dangle down because *gremlins* could grab my fucking ankles at any moment) and I wouldn't dare to get up to go pee, but loving every minute of it and waiting anxiously for the next time that I could be alone in the trailer so I could watch it again and be scared just as much as I was the first time. In the last moments before the credits roll, Hoyt Axton makes a speech that absolutely terrified me. "So, if your air conditioner goes on the fritz, or your washing machine blows up, or your video recorder conks out, before you call the repairman, turn on all the lights, check all the closets and cupboards, look under all the beds, because you never can tell, there might just be a gremlin in your house." Does anyone know how many random noises happen in a trailer? I didn't relax for a year after hearing that speech and it probably shortened my life. It didn't help that I was also all hopped up on Mountain Dew (my mom mistakenly thought it didn't have caffeine because it wasn't a cola) and cheese puffs (which she thought was good for me because they had "cheese" in them). What can I say, it was the 80s. I think eating a loaf of bread while drinking a gallon of milk was considered healthy back then.

Not Being Believed

Another relatable thing about Final Girls, they often aren't believed when they try and tell people that their lives are in danger. Not being believed is a daily fact for most women. When we see this being portrayed on screen it can be validating for women. The fact that we, as the audience, know she is correct to be concerned makes us invested in her being believed. We are often frustrated by the other characters in the film who refuse to believe or support the Final Girl when she needs help. Often in real life scenarios women who ask for help are not believed or are dismissed as being over dramatic. Of course, when these women are later murdered, everyone wonders why nobody did anything to help them.

A lesson I think we can all take away from our Final Girls is that we should believe women more. Movies, and especially genre movies, are only reflections of real life. In real life, women are often the victims of violent crime. In real life, women have to be aware of their surroundings every day. How many men put their car keys between their knuckles when walking through a parking garage to their cars? How many men make sure to open their own bottles and cans of beer when at a house party, or cover their drinks with their hand at a bar to prevent somebody from slipping them a roofie? How many men have been propositioned for prostitution while walking down the street minding their own damn business? These are things that all women are familiar with, because we know that our everyday lives could turn into a real life horror movie at any moment if we're not vigilant, and sometimes even when we are. We can do everything right, and still succumb to violence at the hands of a loved one or stranger. The horror genre reflects that more honestly than any other.

In the early 1980s, many second wave feminists who were protesting the porn industry also protested against horror movies, especially slasher movies. They saw it as reinforcing violence against women. I doubt that very many of these women ever actually watched the movies they were protesting. Although if they did, I don't know that they'd see the things that I see. Movies, art, music, culture as a whole, these are all just Rorschach blots. We see what we want to see, or need to see. I needed to see that being terrified could make you stronger, not weaker. That fear can sometimes forge a scared little girl into a confident woman. Horror movies can often deal with issues that mainstream movies are scared to touch, and although I loved plenty of mainstream movies as a kid, it was the horror movies that gave me hope that I could survive my own terrible circumstances. It let me practice being afraid in a controlled way, it also let me practice being brave. Most of all though, horror can be fun. As part of this lecture I enlisted some female friends of mine to pose as "Final Girls" for a series of photos. Without fail every single girl let me cover them in very sticky fake blood (corn syrup, choco syrup and food coloring), put them out in the cold, and put them through a series of uncomfortable poses. Every single girl told me it was fun—because it *is* fun! I got to make a video to promote an event, and was covered in blood myself. I have to admit there's a strange feeling of power you get while covered in blood, but don't take my word for it, try it for yourself. Have somebody take photos of you as your own Final Girl. Make sure you give yourself a weapon and be creative. Take control over your own narrative! Horror belongs to women more than any other genre, so let's claim it properly and permanently.

MORE JUSTICE AND FEMINISM FROM WWW.MICROCOSM.PUB

SUBSCRIBE!

For as little as $15/month, you can support a small, independent publisher and get every book that we publish—delivered to your doorstep!

www.Microcosm.Pub/BFF

MICROCOSM PUBLISHING is Portland's most diversified publishing house and distributor, with a focus on the colorful, authentic, and empowering. Our books and zines have put your power in your hands since 1996, equipping readers to make positive changes in their lives and in the world around them. Microcosm emphasizes skill-building, showing hidden histories, and fostering creativity through challenging conventional publishing wisdom with books and bookettes about DIY skills, food, bicycling, gender, self-care, and social justice. What was once a distro and record label started by Joe Biel in a drafty bedroom was determined to be *Publishers Weekly*'s fastest-growing publisher of 2022 and #3 in 2023 and 2024, and is now among the oldest independent publishing houses in Portland, OR, and Cleveland, OH. We are a politically moderate, centrist publisher in a world that has inched to the right for the past 80 years.